Cambridge Early Years

Communication and Language

for English as a Second Language

Learner's Book 2B

Claire Medwell

Contents

Note to parents and practitioners   3

Block 3: Working and playing together   4

Block 4: Wonderful water   17

Acknowledgements   32

Note to parents and practitioners

This Learner's Book provides activities to support the second term of ESL Communication and Language for Cambridge Early Years 2.

Activities can be used at school or at home. Children will need support from an adult. Additional guidance about activities can be found in the **For practitioners** boxes.

Stories are provided for children to enjoy looking at and listening to. Children are not expected to be able to read the stories themselves.

Children will encounter the following characters within this book. You could ask children to point to the characters when they see them on the pages, and say their names.

The Learner's Book activities support the Teaching Resource activities. The Teaching Resource provides step-by-step coverage of the Cambridge Early Years curriculum and guidance on how the Learner's Book activities develop the curriculum learning statements.

Hi, my name is Mia.

Find us on the front covers doing lots of fun activities.

Hi, my name is Gemi.

Hi, my name is Rafi.

Hi, my name is Kiho.

Block 3: Working and playing together

Have You Seen Elephant? by David Barrow

1 2 3 4 5 6 7 8 9

... 10!

Coming! Ready or not!

I give up!

There you are!

Hey, what are you playing?

Hide and seek.

Would you like to play tag?

OK.

I must warn you though ...

... I'm VERY good!

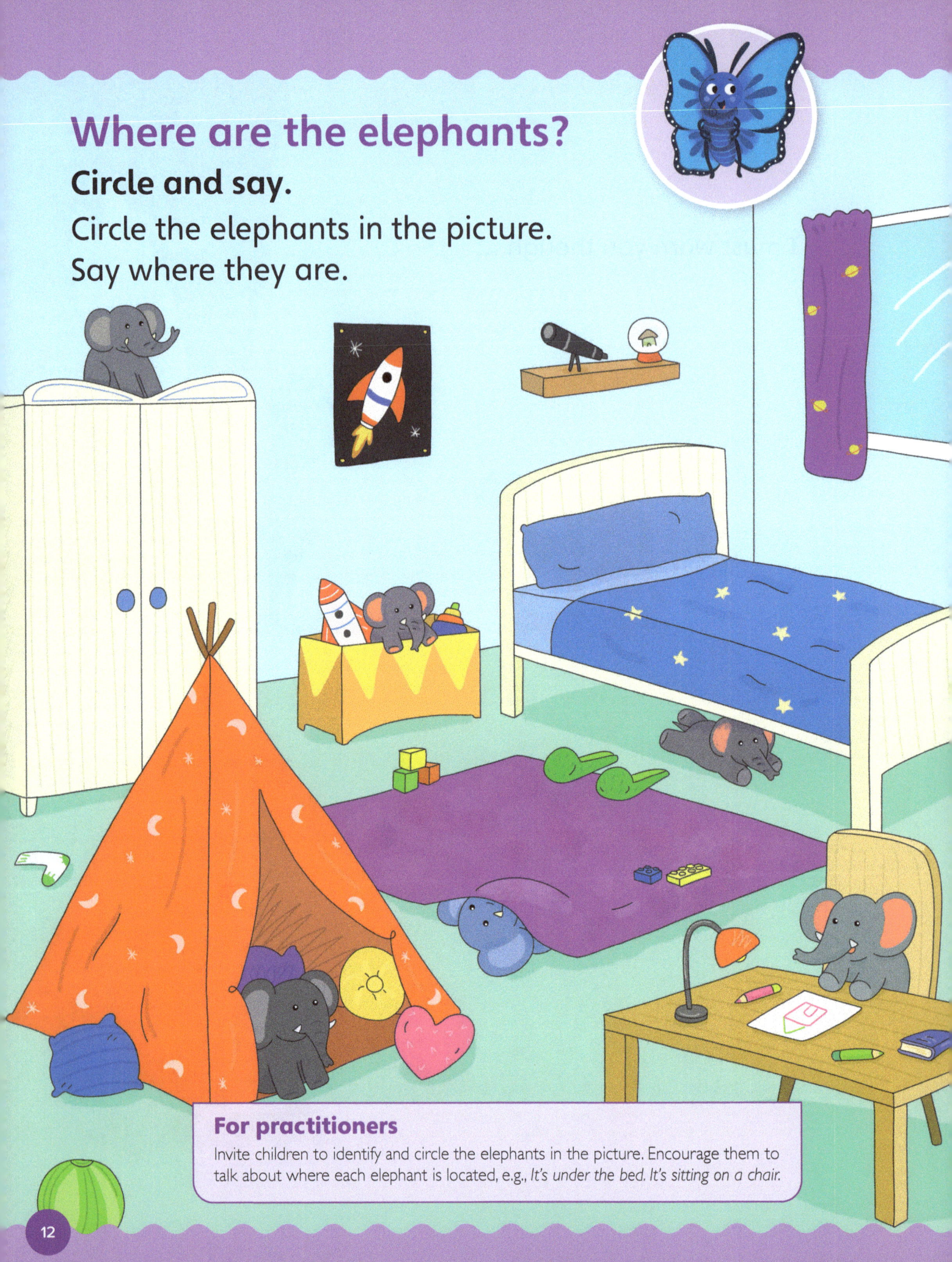

Where are the elephants?

Circle and say.

Circle the elephants in the picture.
Say where they are.

For practitioners
Invite children to identify and circle the elephants in the picture. Encourage them to talk about where each elephant is located, e.g., *It's under the bed. It's sitting on a chair.*

Funny animals

Follow the lines.

Say what each animal is doing.

For practitioners
Invite children to identify each animal in the photos. They then trace each line with their finger to match each photo to a funny picture of the same animal doing different actions. Encourage children to talk about what each animal is doing, e.g., *The elephant is painting.*

What is your favourite toy?

Draw and say.

Draw your favourite toy. Say why it is your favourite.

For practitioners

Encourage children to reflect on the story, *Have You Seen Elephant?*, and invite them to draw their own favourite toy. Ask children to talk about why it is their favourite – what do they like most about it?

In the Playground (to the tune of *Frère Jacques*)

In the playground,
In the playground,
Look at me!
Look at me! *(chorus)*

On the swing, on the swing!
Up and down, up and down.
Repeat chorus

On the slide, on the slide!
Yipeee! Yipeee!
Repeat chorus

On the seesaw, on the seesaw,
Up and down, up and down!
Repeat chorus

On the climbing frame,
On the climbing frame,
Up I go, up I go!
Repeat chorus

In the sandpit, in the sandpit,
Dig, dig, dig!
Dig, dig, dig!

Let's play!

Match and say.

Join each playground object to the correct picture.

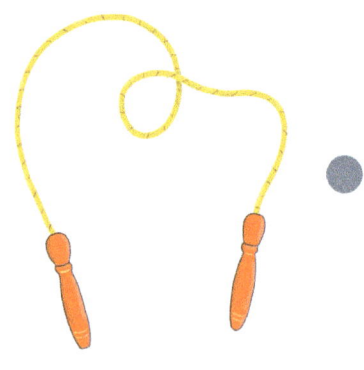

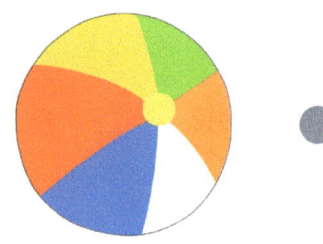

For practitioners
Ask children to identify the playground objects they can see. They then match each to the picture of the game it is used in. Encourage them to talk about which of these games they play themselves, or would like to try.

Block 4 # Wonderful water

We Need Water by Charles Ghigna

See the river. See the lake.

See the puddles raindrops make.

Water helps us all to grow –

every living thing we know.

We save water from the drains ...

... and put out pans each time it rains.

We water all our plants and flowers,

with the water saved from showers.

Every morning, every night,

we turn the tap off, good and tight!

We keep water fresh and clean.

Every river.
Every stream.

Water everywhere!

Join the dots.

Complete the picture to find more water sources.

Can you finish the picture?

For practitioners
Ask children to describe what they can see in the picture. They join the dots to reveal the full picture. Encourage children to talk about all of the water sources they can see.

Water in nature

Colour and say.

Look at the water pictures. Colour in the water words.

rain

river

puddle

sea

For practitioners
Encourage children to explore the pictures of water sources (*rain, river, puddle, sea*). Ask them to trace the water words with their finger as you say them. Now ask them to say the words and then colour them in. Support them as needed.

We need water

Point and say.

Look at the pictures.
Say what each person is doing.

For practitioners
Ask children to describe what is happening in each picture. Encourage them to make connections with their own experiences by talking about how often they do each one.

Old McCrab Had a Sea Farm
(song to the tune of *Old McDonald* ...)

Old McCrab had a sea farm,
EE-I-EE-I-O!
On that farm he had a fish,
EE-I-EE-I-O!
With a swish, swish here,
And a swish, swish there!
Here a swish, there a swish,
Everywhere a swish, swish!
Old McCrab had a sea farm
EE-I-EE-I-O!

More verses: crab *(pinch, pinch)*
shark *(snap, snap)*
octopus *(wiggle, wiggle)*
jelly fish *(blub, blub)*
dolphin *(click, click)*

Lots of animals!

Write and say.
Write the names of the animals. Say each one.

crab

fish

shark

dolphin

jellyfish

octopus

For practitioners
Encourage children to identify, say and write the name of each of the sea animals. Challenge children to use descriptive language to describe some of the animals.

Acknowledgements

The authors and publishers acknowledge the following sources of copyright material and are grateful for the permissions granted. While every effort has been made, it has not always been possible to identify the sources of all the material used, or to trace all copyright holders. If any omissions are brought to our notice, we will be happy to include the appropriate acknowledgements on reprinting.

Have You Seen Elephant? by David Barrow, © Gecko Press

We Need Water by Charles Ghigna, illustrated by Ag Jatcowska, Copyright © 2012 Picture Window Books. All rights reserved. Used with permission from Capstone Publishing, Mankato, Minnesota

Thanks to the following for permission to reproduce images:

p13 Petr Pikora/EyeEm/Getty Images, Gandee Vasan/Getty Images, pepifoto/Getty Images

Thanks to the following artists at Beehive Illustration:

Tamara Joubert, Michelle McGovern, Claire Philpott, Sarah Pitt.

Cover characters by Becky Davies (The Bright Agency)